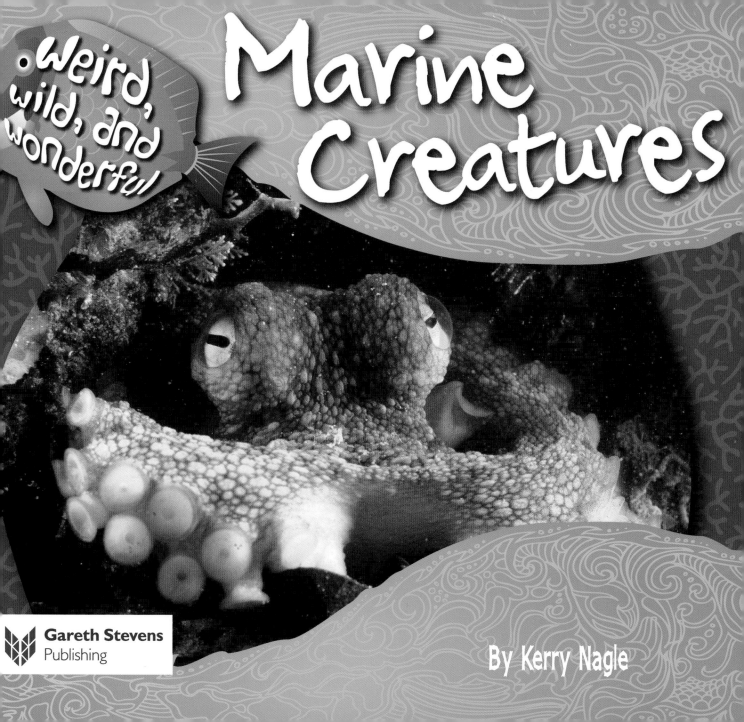

Weird, wild, and wonderful

Marine Creatures

Gareth Stevens
Publishing

By Kerry Nagle

Please visit our Web site **www.garethstevens.com**. For a free color catalog of all our high-quality books, call toll free 1-800-542-2595 or fax 1-877-542-2596.

Library of Congress Cataloging-in-Publication Data

Nagle, Kerry.
 Marine creatures / Kerry Nagle.
    p. cm. — (Weird, wild, and wonderful)
 Includes index.
 ISBN 978-1-4339-3581-7 (library binding)
 1. Marine animals—Juvenile literature. I. Title.
 QL122.2.N237 2010
 591.77—dc22
                                    2009043878

Published in 2010 by
Gareth Stevens Publishing
111 East 14th Street, Suite 349
New York, NY 10003

© 2010 Blake Publishing

For Gareth Stevens Publishing:
Art Direction: Haley Harasymiw
Editorial Direction: Kerri O'Donnell

Designed in Australia by www.design-ed.com.au

Photography by Kathie Atkinson
Additional photographs: © iStockphoto.com/Dale Walsh, p. 4a; © iStockphoto.com/Ron Masessa, p 4b; © iStockphoto.com/Ian Scott, p. 5b; © Paul Banton/Dreamstime.com, p. 6.

Printed in the United States of America

CPSIA compliance information: Batch #CW10GS: For further information contact Gareth Stevens, New York, New York, at 1-800-542-2595.

Contents

Ocean Life

The ocean is a strange and amazing place. Many weird and wonderful animals live there. Some, like seahorses, are tiny. Others, like whales, are the biggest creatures on Earth.

Sea turtles have **flippers** shaped like paddles. This helps them swim.

It's not just fish that live in the ocean. **Mammals,** such as whales, also make their home in the sea.

The ocean has a wide range of **habitats**. Each habitat is special and unusual. The bottom of the ocean is very different from the seashore. Coral reefs are very different from the open sea.

Each habitat has its own animals (and plants) that live there. They are all suited to live in their special home.

In the wild, all animals face the same problems. They must find food and shelter. They must **protect** themselves from being eaten. They must also **breed**.

Special body shapes and parts help animals cope with their **environment**. So do special ways of behaving.

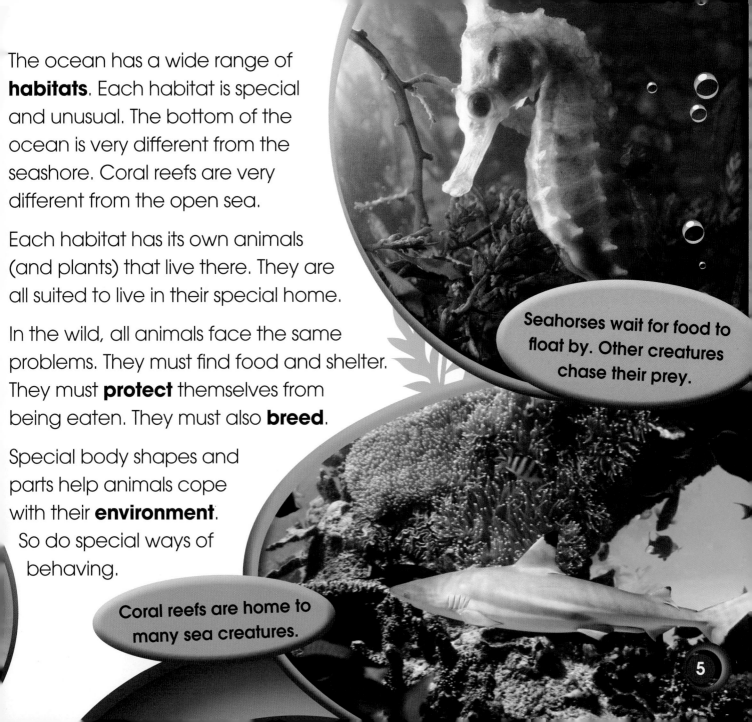

Seahorses wait for food to float by. Other creatures chase their prey.

Coral reefs are home to many sea creatures.

Sharks are fish. They have been around since before dinosaurs. They live in oceans all over the world. Some even live in rivers and lakes.

Sharks have wonderful senses. They can see and hear very well. They can even hear some low sounds that humans can't hear. They also have a sharp sense of smell. Some sharks can smell their **prey** from over a half mile (1 km) away.

Some sharks attack other sharks. This blacktip reef shark was killed by tiger sharks.

Fact Bite

The great white shark has thousands of "spare" teeth. If it loses one of its teeth, a spare will move to the front to take its place.

A great white sh

Sharks have another weird sense, too. All animals give off tiny bits of electricity. Sharks can "feel" this electricity. It helps them track their prey.

Some sharks **hatch** from eggs. Most, though, are born live. Shark parents don't look after their young. All young sharks are on their own from birth.

Some sharks are wild **predators** even before they are born. While still inside the mother, they start to eat each other. Only one or two will live long enough to be born.

The great white shark has very sharp teeth. It rips its food into bits and swallows chunks whole.

7

Fishing for Food

Fish have many clever ways of catching their food.

Moray eels have a wild way of eating. They actually have two sets of jaws. One set is in the mouth. It grabs hold of the prey. The second set is in the throat. These jaws reach forward and pull the prey down the throat so it can be swallowed.

Frogfish stay very still to catch their food. When a crab, shrimp, or octopus passes by, they pounce. They open their mouths wide and swallow the prey whole!

These moray eels are waiting for dinner to swim by.

Fact Bite

Moray eels move their bodies in a wave motion. They can swim backwards as well as forwards.

An anglerfish dangles its "bait" in front of its open mouth.

Sawfish have a weird **snout** that looks like a saw. They use it to **stun** their prey with blows.

When anglerfish want food, they go fishing! Females have a fin that looks like a fishing rod with bait at the end. The anglerfish waves the bait around. Its prey thinks the bait is a tasty treat. It comes closer. In a flash, the anglerfish sucks its prey into its big mouth.

The frogfish has a big head, a wide mouth, and a "beard."

The teeth on the sawfish's saw are razor sharp.

9

This seahorse is hiding in seaweed.

The wonderful seahorse is very different from other fish. It is covered with bony **armor**, not scales. The top of the head is shaped like a crown. This is called a coronet.

The seahorse's long snout is like a tube. When food swims by, the snout sucks it up—just like a vacuum cleaner!

The seahorse is a slow swimmer. It uses its curled tail to hold on to seaweed. This stops it from getting swept away by wild sea currents.

Seahorses can change color. This helps them hide from their enemies. They also change color to send messages.

Most seahorses **mate** for life. Each morning, the female swims over to her **mate**. They both change color. Next, they do a special dance. Then they swim off and go about their daily tasks.

A weird thing about the seahorse is that the male has the babies! The male keeps the female's eggs inside his body. The babies hatch. Then they come out of his pouch.

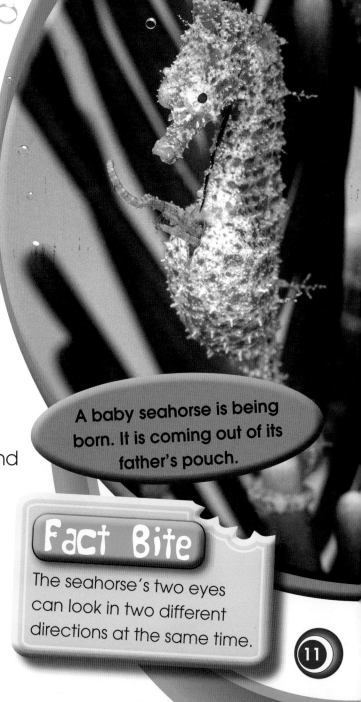

A baby seahorse is being born. It is coming out of its father's pouch.

Fact Bite

The seahorse's two eyes can look in two different directions at the same time.

Monster Shells

You can often find empty shells on the beach. They were once the homes of sea snails.

Balers are sea snails. They have some of the biggest shells of all. Their wonderful, glossy shells have beautiful patterns.

A huge baler shell on Barrow Island, Western Australia

Balers are wild **carnivores**. They eat small marine animals (even other sea snails).

Balers crawl around on a weird, large foot. Some balers also use this foot to catch prey.

A baler has a soft tube that sticks out from under its shell. Water is sucked in through the tube. The baler "tastes" the water to check for food nearby.

This baler has pulled its foot and its tube into its shell.

This baler is crawling on the sand. Its tube is poking out in front.

13

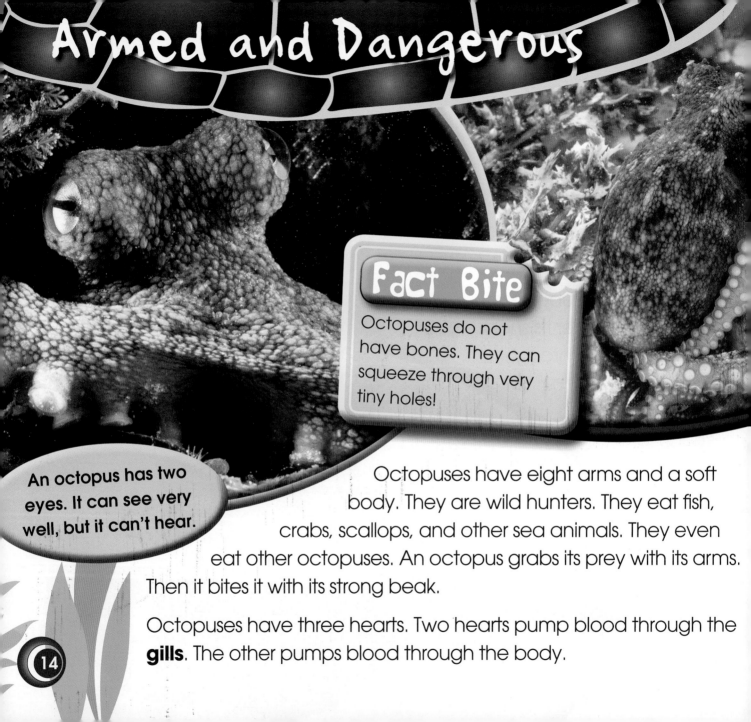

Armed and Dangerous

An octopus has two eyes. It can see very well, but it can't hear.

Octopuses have eight arms and a soft body. They are wild hunters. They eat fish, crabs, scallops, and other sea animals. They even eat other octopuses. An octopus grabs its prey with its arms. Then it bites it with its strong beak.

Octopuses have three hearts. Two hearts pump blood through the **gills**. The other pumps blood through the body.

The octopus hunts at night.

The octopus protects itself in wonderful ways. It squirts black "ink" into the water when it is scared. This hides the octopus so it can escape from enemies. The octopus can change color to help it blend in to its surroundings. It can also drop off an arm if it is attacked.

Octopuses move slowly. They crawl or swim. However, sometimes they need to move fast. They send a burst of water through a tube called a siphon. This shoots them through the water like a jet!

The octopus has suction cups on its arms. They are used to "taste" what they touch.

Octopuses live in holes under rocks.

15

Small and Deadly

Fact Bite

Most octopuses hunt at night. The blue-ring octopus hunts during the day.

The blue-ring octopus is small—but deadly. It is the most **poisonous** octopus in the world. It lives in the oceans off Australia.

This octopus has blue rings on each of its eight arms. When it feels scared, the blue rings light up. That's a warning to others: "I'm wild—stay away!"

The octopus has two types of poison. One poison is used on its prey. This poison stops the prey from moving. The other poison defends the octopus from attack. This poison can kill a human.

The blue rings on the octopus light up when it is in danger.

Sometimes, the octopus bites and poisons its prey. Sometimes, it shoots poison into the water. The poison is soaked up by the prey.

The female octopus carries her eggs under her arms. She is a wonderful mother. She looks after her eggs very carefully. She sprays water over them to clean them. After the eggs hatch, the mother dies. The baby octopuses must take care of themselves.

This octopus is hiding near a rock. It will pounce on the crab when it comes nearer.

The octopus sucks out the crab's soft body to eat. It leaves the shell.

Long-Distance Swimmers

Marine turtles are **reptiles**. They have lived in the oceans for over 100 million years. They have a large shell. They also have a small head and four strong flippers.

Green turtles live in the Atlantic and Pacific oceans. They are wonderful swimmers. They feed in the ocean but make their nests on land. It can be a very long way between the two places.

This female is leaving the sea. It is time for her to dig her nest in the sand.

The turtle drags herself up the beach. She is going to dig a nest and lay her eggs. You can see the tracks of other females in the sand.

When it is time to lay their eggs, the females leave the sea. They dig a hole in the sand with their flippers. They lay their eggs in the hole. They cover the eggs with sand. Then they go back to the sea.

After 64 days, the eggs hatch. The sex of a baby turtle depends on how hot the sand is. Eggs laid in hotter sand turn into females. Males hatch from eggs laid in cooler sand. Weird!

The newborn turtle must trek down to the sea. This is a dangerous time. Birds and crabs feed on the young turtles on the beach. In the water, sharks are waiting for them. Many young turtles die at this time.

A female turtle fills in her nest.

Fact Bite

Young green turtles eat meat. Adults eat plants, such as seagrass and seaweed.

This baby green turtle has just hatched out of its egg. It digs its way through the sand. Then it makes its way down the beach to the sea.

Flippers and Fur

Sea lions are mammals. They live on shore but feed in the ocean. In the water, they are fast and graceful. Their front flippers speed them along. The back ones are used for steering. On land, sea lions move about on all four flippers.

The water where sea lions live can be very cold. They have two layers of fur to keep them warm. They also have a layer of fat, called blubber. Out of the water, they love to soak up the sun.

Sea lions love to surf!

Young sea lions playing in the sun

Sea lions like to live in groups called colonies. Most of the time, they are friendly and playful. But at breeding time, male sea lions often fight each other. They make weird barking and growling sounds at each other. They want to be in charge of as many females as they can.

Australian sea lions are very rare. In the past, people hunted them. Now, they are protected by law. There are about 10,000 of them in the wild.

Sea lion babies are called pups. This one is sleeping. Its mother will feed and protect it for about a year.

A sea lion colony

Fact Bites

Sea lions have small ears.

Sea lions can hold their breath for a long time. They can dive and swim in very deep water. But they still need to come to the surface to get air.

Fact File: Special Features

Animals that live in the sea come in all shapes and sizes. Some have scales, some have fur. Some have a backbone, some don't. Some are born live, some hatch from eggs. Some are fast swimmers. Others move about slowly. But they all have one thing in common. Their bodies and how they act are suited to their ocean home.

Special Features							
Animal	**Fins**	**Scales**	**Fur**	**Back-bone**	**Shell**	**Live young**	**Lays eggs**
great white shark	✓	✓		✓		✓	
sea lion			✓	✓		✓	
baler					✓		✓
octopus							✓
seahorse	✓			✓			✓
anglerfish	✓	✓		✓			✓
green turtle				✓	✓		✓
moray eel	✓			✓			✓

Glossary

armor   tough, hard covering that protects you from being hurt

breed   to have babies

carnivores   animals that eat meat

environment   all the living and nonliving things where an animal lives

flippers   broad, flat legs used for swimming

gills   the organs many sea creatures breathe through

habitats   the natural surroundings where animals or plants usually live

hatch   to come out of an egg

mammals   warm-blooded animals with hair, fur, whiskers, or bristles. They feed their young on mother's milk.

mate (a)   a partner that you have babies with

mate (to)   to make babies

poisonous   able to kill you or make you sick if you take it in

predators   animals that hunt, kill, and eat other animals

prey   an animal that is hunted and killed for food by another animal

protect   keep safe from being hunted

reptile   an animal that breathes air using lungs, whose body is covered with scales, and whose blood changes temperature depending on its environment

snout   a long nose

stun   to stop an animal from being able to act because it has been hurt

For Further Information

Books

Pipe, Jim. *Scary Creatures of the Deep*. New York: Franklin Watts, 2009.

Yount, Lisa. *Modern Marine Science: Exploring the Deep*. New York: Chelsea House Publications, 2006.

Web Sites

Marine Life Kid's Corner
http://www.fishid.com/facts.htm

SOS for Kids
http://www.saveourseas.com/minisites/kids/82.html

Publisher's note to educators and parents: Our editors have carefully reviewed these Web sites to ensure that they are suitable for students. Many Web sites change frequently, however, and we cannot guarantee that a site's future contents will continue to meet our high standards of quality and educational value. Be advised that students should be closely supervised whenever they access the Internet.

Index